12/21

U.S. Government
Q&A!

How Are LAWS Made?

By Julia McDonnell

Gareth Stevens
PUBLISHING

Please visit our website, www.garethstevens.com. For a free color catalog of all our high-quality books, call toll free 1-800-542-2595 or fax 1-877-542-2596.

Library of Congress Cataloging-in-Publication Data

Names: McDonnell, Julia, 1979- author.
Title: How are laws made? / Julia McDonnell.
Description: New York : Gareth Stevens Publishing, 2022. | Series: U.S. government Q & A! | Includes index.
Identifiers: LCCN 2020033496 (print) | LCCN 2020033497 (ebook) | ISBN 9781538264157 (library binding) | ISBN 9781538264133 (paperback) | ISBN 9781538264140 (set) | ISBN 9781538264164 (ebook)
Subjects: LCSH: Legislation–United States–Juvenile literature. | Legislative bodies–United States–Juvenile literature. | Bill drafting–United States–Juvenile literature. | Legislation–United States–History–Juvenile literature.
Classification: LCC KF4945 .M398 2022 (print) | LCC KF4945 (ebook) | DDC 328.73/077–dc23
LC record available at https://lccn.loc.gov/2020033496
LC ebook record available at https://lccn.loc.gov/2020033497

First Edition

Published in 2022 by
Gareth Stevens Publishing
29 E. 21st Street
New York, NY 10010

Designer: Andrea Davison-Bartolotta
Editor: Charlie Light

Photo credits: Cover Alexander Supertramp/Shutterstock.com; series art (paper, feather) Incomible/Shutterstock.com; series art (blue banner, red banner, stars) pingbat/Shutterstock.com; p. 5 courtesy of National Archives; p. 7 Wikimedia Commons/File:Scene_at_the_Signing_of_the_Constitution_of_the_United_States.jpg; p. 9 Wikimedia Commons/File: 111th US Senate class photo.jpg; pp. 11 (main), 17 (main) courtesy of Library of Congress; pp. 11 (pins), 17 (pins) Alexander Limbach/Shutterstock.com; p. 13 Mark Makela/Getty Images; p. 15 Chip Somodevilla/Getty Images; p. 19 Saul Loeb/AFP via Getty Images; p. 20 Zurijeta/Shutterstock.com; p. 21 KindheartedStock/Shutterstock.com.

Printed in the United States of America

Some of the images in this book illustrate individuals who are models. The depictions do not imply actual situations or events.

CPSIA compliance information: Batch #CSGS22: For further information contact Gareth Stevens, New York, New York at 1-800-542-2595.

Find us on

Contents

Words in the glossary appear in **bold** type the first time they are used in the text.

What Is a Law?

You may not realize it, but laws touch just about every part of your life. A law is a rule that the government makes. Laws try to either solve a problem or stop a problem from happening. A law could be made for almost any reason you can think of, like keeping **citizens** and natural areas safe, or helping the government work properly.

How does a simple idea become an actual law? The United States Congress takes care of that!

★ ★ ★ ★ ★ ★ ★ ★ ★ ★ ★ ★

Government Guides

"Our Constitution works; our great **republic** is a government of laws and not of men. Here, the people rule."
– Gerald R. Ford,
38th U.S. President

Article I, which sets the rules for Congress, fills up around half of the Constitution! The Constitution is the piece of writing that states U.S. laws. That shows how much thought the framers put into making laws and **representation**.

Who Will Be in Charge?

The **American Revolution** ended in 1783. In 1787, over 50 men called the framers met in Philadelphia to build a new government for the young nation. They knew that whoever was in charge of making the laws would have a lot of responsibility—which means a lot of power.

The framers decided the government would have three branches. One branch would be a **legislature** called Congress. Its members would be elected by the American people. The framers hoped Congress would pass laws with their fellow citizens in mind.

★ ★ ★ ★ ★ ★ ★ ★ ★ ★ ★ ★ ★

Government Guides

"We have the oldest written constitution still in force in the world, and it starts out with three words: 'We, the people.'"
– Supreme Court Justice Ruth Bader Ginsburg

George Washington led the Constitution's framers. The U.S. Constitution set the country on a new path after the failure of the Articles of Confederation, the nation's first constitution, by creating a more powerful central government.

It Begins with an Idea

Congress is made of two **chambers**: the Senate and the House of Representatives. Each state has two senators. The more people who live in a state, the more representatives it has.

Laws begin as bills. The idea for a bill can come from anyone—even you! Citizens who want to see a change can reach out to their representatives or senators about it. After looking into the idea, that member of Congress might write it into a bill. Either chamber can introduce, or share, a bill.

★ ★ ★ ★ ★ ★ ★ ★ ★ ★ ★ ★ ★

Government Guides

"In the face of impossible odds, people who love this country can change it."
– Barack Obama,
44th U.S. President

Each of the 100 senators has their own desk. The person leading the Senate that day sits on top of the dais, or small stage, at the head of the chamber.

The First Step in Congress

A bill needs support as it makes its way through Congress. At least one member must **sponsor** the bill. Then the bill can be introduced to the rest of the members of the sponsor's chamber. That way everyone understands what the bill is about.

It would be too much work for every member to work on every bill. The House Speaker or Senate **Parliamentarian** sends the bill to a **committee**. Members of Congress belong to committees based on their skills and knowledge. Most bills don't make it past committees.

★ ★ ★ ★ ★ ★ ★ ★ ★ ★ ★ ★

Government Guides

"Whenever the people are well informed, they can be trusted with their own government."
– Thomas Jefferson, 3rd U.S. President

Representatives officially introduce their bills by putting them in the hopper (a wooden box), just as Texas Rep. Maury Maverick does in this photo from the late 1930s.

11

The Job of Committees

The committee looks at the bill more closely. The committee can make a smaller group called a subcommittee to find more information about the bill's subject. They get this information from government offices, **experts**, and public hearings.

The subcommittee takes what they learned back to the committee. The committee can then amend, or change, the bill. They can combine it with another bill. Or they can agree it wouldn't make a good law—or wouldn't get enough votes. In the last two cases, they will let it "die" or end.

★ ★ ★ ★ ★ ★ ★ ★ ★ ★ ★ ★

Government Guides

"[Democracy] is not about making speeches. It is about making committees work."
– Alan Bullock,
British Historian

The House Ways and Means Committee holds a hearing in March 2020. It's the oldest committee in the House. It works on bills about taxes.

13

Yes or No?

Bills that make it past committee go back to the chamber floor. All members can share what they think about the bill. Senators can filibuster, or make a long speech to hold off more action. One senator "filibustered" for over 24 hours straight! More amendments, or changes, can be made to the bill. Finally, it's ready to be voted on!

Representatives vote by saying "aye," "no," or "present" out loud. Aye means yes and present means the member isn't taking sides. Members can also vote by standing and being counted, or using electronic stations. Senators usually vote by saying "yea" or "nay."

During this 2019 vote in the House of Representatives, the names of the members are displayed.

Government Guides

"Congress is where Americans are supposed to have our big, messy political [government-connected] fights."
– Ben Sasse,
Senator from Nebraska

If the majority of House or Senate members vote for the bill, the process starts all over again in the other chamber! It takes 218 votes to pass in the House and 51 to pass in the Senate.

If both chambers pass a bill but one chamber has made changes to it, a new committee of House and Senate members work together to fix any differences. The committee members write a report on the changes for their chamber. If both chambers approve the report, the bill goes to the president. Otherwise, the bill dies.

★ ★ ★ ★ ★ ★ ★ ★ ★ ★ ★

Government Guides

"...the American system of government requires that the sense of the majority should prevail [succeed]."
– Alexander Hamilton, American statesman

This photo from 1938 shows Senator Elbert Thomas of Utah and Representative Mary Norton of New Jersey talking about the Wage and Hour bill, which aimed to help improve American working standards.

17

What Does the President Think?

The president can do one of three things:

(1) Sign the bill, making it a law.

(2) **Veto** it. This sends it back to Congress. If the two chambers still think it should be a law, they vote again. If two-thirds of each chamber vote to pass the bill, it becomes a law.

(3) Do nothing. If Congress is in **session** at the time, it becomes a law after 10 days. If Congress stops meeting within the 10 days, it's a "pocket veto," meaning the bill dies.

★ ★ ★ ★ ★ ★ ★ ★ ★ ★ ★ ★

Government Guides

"Officeholders are the agents [people who act on behalf of others] of the people, not their masters."
– Grover Cleveland,
22nd and 24th U.S. President

President Obama signs a financial bill into law in 2010. Members of Congress and regular citizens are often invited to be a part of the moment.

From 1789 Through Today

Congress has made thousands of laws since it first met in 1789. Some laws have helped the American people or given them more rights. Other laws have taken away freedoms or caused harm to certain groups of people. Luckily, our government can pass new laws to fix the mistakes of earlier ones.

Members of Congress are elected to be "the voice of the people." But you can speak up too! What laws do you think we need?

★ ★ ★ ★ ★ ★ ★ ★ ★ ★ ★ ★ ★

Think About It!

If you could introduce any bill to Congress, what would it be? Do you think it would have a good chance of turning into a law?

How a Bill Becomes a Law

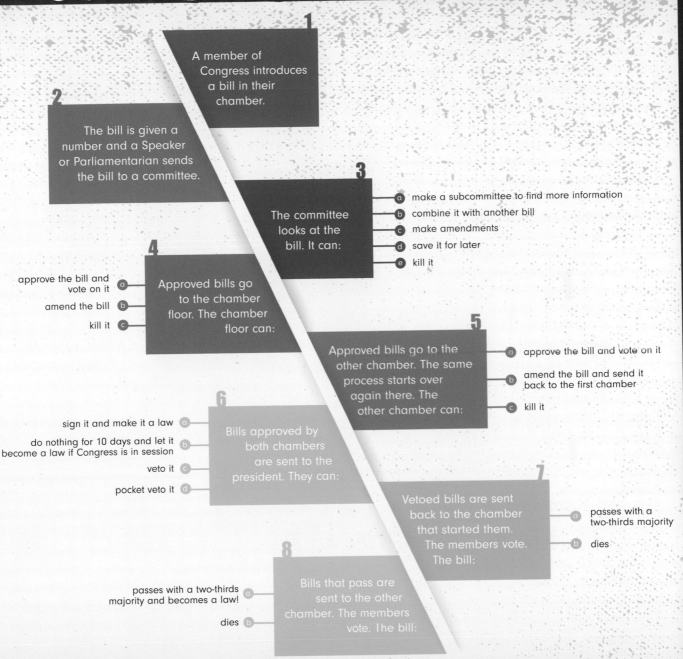

1 A member of Congress introduces a bill in their chamber.

2 The bill is given a number and a Speaker or Parliamentarian sends the bill to a committee.

3 The committee looks at the bill. It can:
- a make a subcommittee to find more information
- b combine it with another bill
- c make amendments
- d save it for later
- e kill it

4 Approved bills go to the chamber floor. The chamber floor can:
- a approve the bill and vote on it
- b amend the bill
- c kill it

5 Approved bills go to the other chamber. The same process starts over again there. The other chamber can:
- a approve the bill and vote on it
- b amend the bill and send it back to the first chamber
- c kill it

6 Bills approved by both chambers are sent to the president. They can:
- a sign it and make it a law
- b do nothing for 10 days and let it become a law if Congress is in session
- c veto it
- d pocket veto it

7 Vetoed bills are sent back to the chamber that started them. The members vote. The bill:
- a passes with a two-thirds majority
- b dies

8 Bills that pass are sent to the other chamber. The members vote. The bill:
- a passes with a two-thirds majority and becomes a law!
- b dies

Glossary

American Revolution: the war in which the colonies won their freedom from England

chamber: a group of people who form part of a country's government

citizen: someone who lives in a country legally and has certain rights

committee: a group of people who are picked to do a specific job or to make decisions about something

expert: someone who knows a great deal about something

legislature: a lawmaking body

Parliamentarian: someone who knows a lot about the rules of their chamber and the rules of making laws. There is one Parliamentarian in the House and one in the Senate.

representation: having to do with a person or group of people who speak or act for another person or group

republic: a form of government in which the people elect representatives who run the government

session: a meeting of an official group

sponsor: to take responsibility for something

veto: to reject a proposed law officially or to refuse to allow a bill to become a law

For More Information

Books

Bandy, Michael S. and Eric Stein. *Granddaddy's Turn: A Journey to the Ballot Box.* Somerville, MA: Candlewick Press, 2019.

McDaniel, Melissa. *The U.S. Congress: Why It Matters to You.* New York, NY: Children's Press, an imprint of Scholastic, 2020.

Roosevelt, Eleanor and Michelle Markel. *When You Grow Up to Vote: How Our Government Works for You.* New York, NY: Roaring Brook Press, 2018.

Websites

KidCitizen
www.kidcitizen.net
Interactive lessons and historical sources from the Library of Congress guide you through the government and the important role citizens have.

Kids in the House
kids-clerk.house.gov
Explore the history and importance of the House of Representatives—and take a photo tour of its chamber in the Capitol building—through this website run by its Office of the Clerk.

U.S. Government: How Laws Are Made
www.ducksters.com/history/us_government/how_laws_are_made.php
Dig deeper into the lawmaking process at this kid-friendly site.

Index